BRITAIN'S STORY

TOLD IN PICTURES

OVER 450 ILLUSTRATIONS DEPICTING THE
HISTORY OF BRITAIN FROM THE EARLIEST
———— TIMES TO THE PRESENT DAY ————

Copyright.

[*On cover:* ... *By C. H. Aime*]

MANCHESTER :
SANKEY, HUDSON & CO.

Printed in England.

1. PREHISTORIC BRITAIN.

The Prehistoric Age covers the whole period of time prior to the Roman Occupation of Britain (43 A.D. The life then active has little bearing on History proper; it serves chiefly as an introduction indicating th cultural stages through which Man slowly rose to Civilisation. During the Prehistoric Age Britain was in habited successively by the Palaeolithic or Old Stone Age Men, the Neolithic or New Stone Age Men an the Celts, frequently called the Ancient Britons.

Palaeolithic Men were brutal, nomadic aborigines who subsisted entirely upon the wild animals the hunted. Nevertheless, succeeding generations present distinctive pictures of human progress, the later an more advanced types being the many races of Cave Men who achieved a rude family and social life, ma weapons, utensils and implements from flint, bone and horn, wore the skins of animals as clothing and use fire for warmth and cooking. The weapons in use were flint knives and daggers, and horn or bone land heads and harpoons both plain and barbed, and though these were effective against small game, large anim like the elk, reindeer, woolly rhinoceros and mammoth had to be trapped. The common implements we large, pear-shaped flints roughly chipped and used for digging, keen-edged flint slivers or flakes for cuttin and scrapers and borers of service in the preparation of skins and the manufacture of weapons.

A surprising feature of the Cave culture is the artistic skill expressed by craftsmen, notably in well-defin animal forms etched on bone, carved from stone and ivory and painted in colours on pebbles and cave wal Well known cave dwellings are at Cresswell Crags, Derbyshire, Wookey Hole, Cheddar, Kent's Cave Torquay, and the Paviland Cave, South Wales.

The Neolithic Men advanced greatly in civilisation. Their characteristic stone weapons were well shape ground and polished and bored for hafting. They were not nomads, but herdsmen and farmers living chie on the hill slopes where they cultivated wheat, barley and flax, reared domestic animals, notably the co sheep, goat and dog, and carried on such industries as pottery-making, building, spinning and weavin Their community or social sense is expressed in their entrenched and palisaded villages of wattled huts, th hill forts and strong-holds and their dwellings erected on piles over shallow water. Also, their knowled of religion is indicated by their care for the dead whom they buried in long mounds called barrows, and their stone circles or temples the largest being those at Avebury and Stonehenge.

The Celts were a tall people with light hair and eyes who invaded Britain from Gaul. The earlier vaders, later known as Goidels or Gaels, introduced bronze and settled chiefly in the north and west. I later invaders, who appeared about 400 B.C., were the Brythons or Britons who introduced iron and we more advanced in the arts of life and government.

The Britons enjoyed a well organised tribal government under civil chiefs influenced by religious lead who as druids, bards and magicians exercised great power. They settled in fortified villages around wh they carried on agriculture and horse and cattle rearing. In certain districts they mined and smelted met chiefly copper, tin and iron. Also, pottery, glass, linen and woollen cloths were manufactured, while me weapons, implements and utensils, ornamented and beautified, were made in great variety.

A notable feature in British progress was the growth of trade, communication and transport being ma tained between tribal centres by well-defined trackways and, on the rivers, by heavy, dug-out canoes light wicker coracles. As early as 300 B.C. the Britons traded with Phoenician merchants from Cartha and there was a steady export of corn, hides, dogs and copper to Gaul. Early trade was by barter, but la money was used; at first as iron bars, subsequently as rough coins.

2

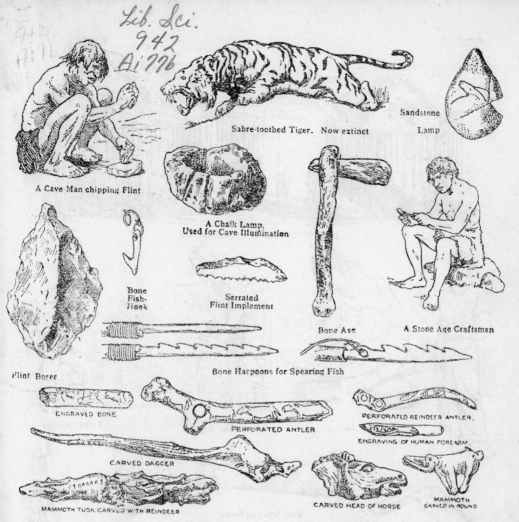

A Cave Man chipping Flint

Sabre-toothed Tiger. Now extinct

Sandstone Lamp

A Chalk Lamp.
Used for Cave Illumination

Bone Fish-Hook

Serrated Flint Implement

Bone Axe

A Stone Age Craftsman

Flint Borer

Bone Harpoons for Spearing Fish

ENGRAVED BONE

PERFORATED ANTLER

PERFORATED REINDEER ANTLER.

ENGRAVING OF HUMAN FOREARM.

CARVED DAGGER

MAMMOTH TUSK CARVED WITH REINDEER

CARVED HEAD OF HORSE

MAMMOTH CARVED IN ROUND

Art Products of the Cave Men in Bone and Horn

Musk-sheep.
Now an Arctic Animal

Flint Hand-axe

Woolly Rhinoceros. Now extinct

3

Typical Pile-dwellings of the Neolithic Age

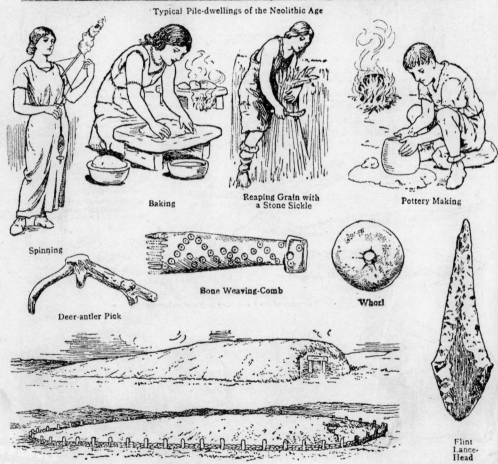

Spinning

Baking

Reaping Grain with
a Stone Sickle

Pottery Making

Deer-antler Pick

Bone Weaving-Comb

Whorl

Flint
Lance-
Head

Late Neolithic Long Barrows or Burial Mounds

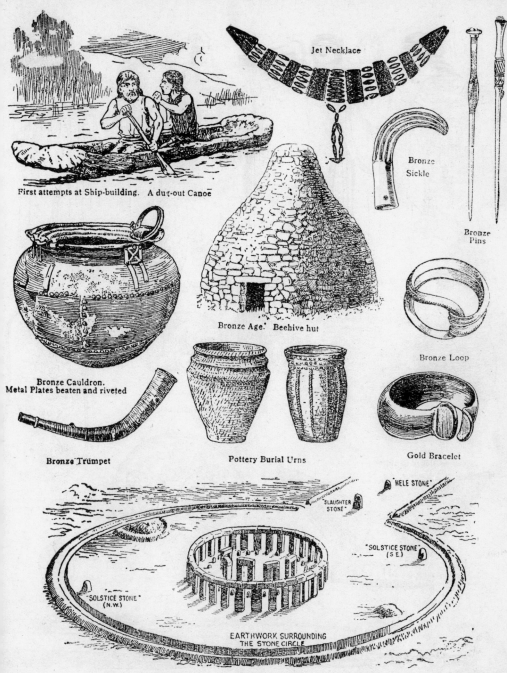

First attempts at Ship-building. A dug-out Canoe

Jet Necklace

Bronze Sickle

Bronze Pins

Bronze Age. Beehive hut

Bronze Loop

Bronze Cauldron.
Metal Plates beaten and riveted

Bronze Trumpet

Pottery Burial Urns

Gold Bracelet

HELE STONE

SLAUGHTER STONE

SOLSTICE STONE (S.E.)

SOLSTICE STONE (N.W.)

EARTHWORK SURROUNDING
THE STONE CIRCLE

A Reconstruction of the Neolithic Age Stone Circle at Stonehenge, Salisbury Plain

British Chief

British Bard

British Chief in War Dress

British Druid

Bronze Cauldron

Bronze Harness Ornament

Bronze Shield with Enamel Ornament

Bronze Helmet

Back of Decorated Bronze Mirror

Celtic Iron Sword

Decorated Scabbards

6

2. ROMAN BRITAIN. A.D. 43-410.

The Romans first made a brief contact with the Britons through the punitive expeditions under Julius Caesar in B.C. 55 and 54. "In Britain," wrote Caesar, "the population is large, the houses numerous and cattle abundant. The people of Kent are the most civilised. They are splendid horsemen, and fight also from chariots."

In 43 A.D. the Conquest of Britain was ordered by the Emperor Claudius, a long and costly campaign since, owing to the fierce resistance of the hill tribes of the west and north, it occupied a period of nearly forty years. In A.D. 61, a crisis was reached by the revolt of the Iceni (East Anglia) who, under Boudicca, succeeded in destroying the rising cities of Colchester, St. Albans and London before their rising was suppressed by Seutonius. Following this revolt the Conquest was completed by various commanders of whom the ablest was Julius Agricola (78-85). He subdued the north, conciliated the south and established Britain as a Roman Province. Throughout the Roman Period (A.D. 43-410) civil administration was effective only in the Lowland areas of the Midlands, east and south. The west and north formed a military area occupied by large bodies of troops garrisoning the three great legionary cities of York, Chester and Caerleon, numerous secondary forts, and the Northern Wall which, built by the Emperor Hadrian in 120 as a defence against the Picts of Caledonia, ran across country for seventy miles from the Solway Firth to the mouth of the Tyne.

Politically, Roman rule checked British national developement, but civilisation was greatly fostered, chiefly by the introduction of settled government and superior laws. Agriculture was so improved that by the third century corn became the chief export. Mining was increased, notably the mining of lead in Somerset and Shropshire, copper and tin in Cornwall and iron in Sussex and the Forest of Dean. In addition, existing industries, such as spinning, weaving and dyeing were extended, and the establishment of new industries such as pottery and glass making gave further scope to Celtic skill in craftsmanship.

Britain attracted large numbers of Roman settlers, artisans, manufacturers and merchants, but her prosperity was assured by the rapid growth in trade. Externally, the vast Roman Empire lay open to British commerce. Internally, trade was fostered by the rise of towns and cities, by the needs of the large military population and by the laying down of a system of magnificent roads communicating with all parts of the Province. Owing to its situation, London, which became the "brain" of Roman Britain, early rose to supreme importance as a commercial, industrial and administrative centre. The government of the towns was mainly left to councils comprising the chief citizens, the duties of local bodies, besides the administration of justice, including such municipal functions as water supply, drainage, markets, and police.

The Romans introduced their own religious cults into Britain, temples in the towns being dedicated to their various gods, notably Jupiter, Juno and Minerva. Later, Christianity gained many adherents in Britain, and the traces of an organised British Church, though few, are distinct.

After A.D. 250 Britain suffered so severely from the raids of Saxon pirates that the East Coast had to be garrisoned and fortified. A century later the whole empire was so beset by barbarian tribes that Britain was steadily stripped of its regular defences until in 410 the Roman Occupation was ended by the withrawal of the last legions for the defence of Rome.

Apart from the ruins of Hadrian's Wall the most interesting Roman remains in Britain are the comfortable houses or villas scattered throughout the countryside. Such villas were the centres of extensive and well-organised estates. Within them well-to-do Britons provided for numerous dependants and lived luxurious lives. Around them were peasants and labourers who dwelt in cottages heated by hypocausts and roofed with Roman tiles, and who, in their daily lives, dressed well and comfortably, spoke Latin, and used Roman plate and pottery. It is noteworthy too, that the villas, and they are especially numerous in Kent, Sussex, Hampshire and Essex, are all Celtic in plan, but their fittings, that is, their hypocausts, mosaics, baths and decorations are all Roman.

Of Roman London or Londinium, History tells but a meagre tale. How the city was founded we do not know, but it was prominent very soon after 43 A.D. as an essential commercial and distributing centre for the new Province. In 61 A.D. the settlement was burnt by Boudicca, but it grew so steadily after it was rebuilt that all the Roman remains found beneath its present surface prove its immense prosperity. In addition to its fine Basilica, London contained many public buildings such as temples and baths, but little is known of them. Outside the city, near the Newgate, was the Amphitheatre where on holidays the whole populace gave itself up to the excitement of chariot racing and gladiatorial fights. Near the Strand may still be seen a bathroom entirely lined with marble. Altars dedicated to gods and goddesses tell us of many Roman shrines and temples, and a few small objects marked with Christian symbols speak of the existence in later times of christian churches. The best known relic of Roman London is the famous London Stone now preserved in the wall of St. Swithin's, Cannon Street.

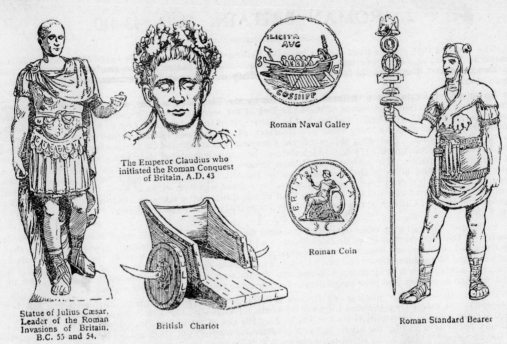

Statue of Julius Cæsar, Leader of the Roman Invasions of Britain, B.C. 55 and 54.

The Emperor Claudius who initiated the Roman Conquest of Britain, A.D. 43

Roman Naval Galley

Roman Coin

British Chariot

Roman Standard Bearer

The Roman Legions under Cæsar land at Walmer Beach, B.C. 55.

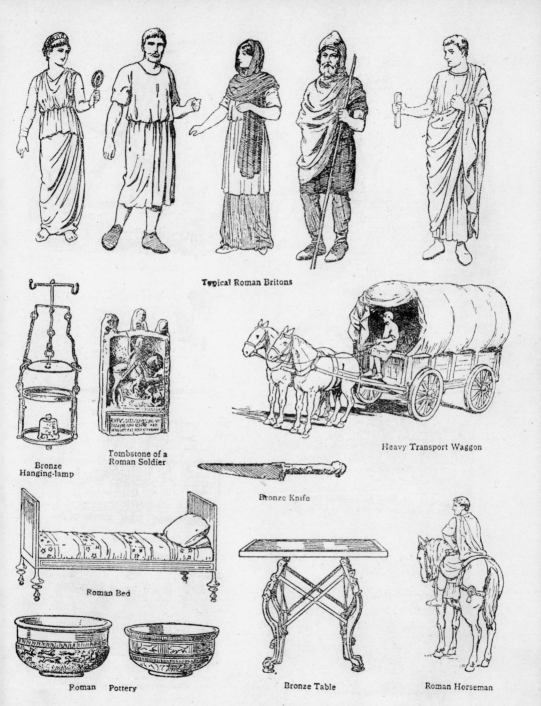

Typical Roman Britons

Bronze
Hanging-lamp

Tombstone of a
Roman Soldier

Heavy Transport Waggon

Bronze Knife

Roman Bed

Roman   Pottery

Bronze Table

Roman Horseman

9

Roman Naval Galley

Roman Catapult

The Northern Wall. Built by the Emperor Hadrian,
A.D. 120. to withstand attacks of the Picts

Roman Chariot

Battering Ram

The Multangular Tower, York.
A fine example of Roman Masonry

A Roman Gateway with
characteristic semi-circular arch

10

3. ANGLO-SAXON BRITAIN. 410-1066.

The English are descended from the Angles, Saxons and Jutes, kindred Teutonic tribes originally inhabiting Northern Germany and Denmark. In the early 3rd century they first raided the British coasts. Their descents became more common as the Roman power declined until the withdrawal of the legions led them to embark upon a definite and successful policy of conquest and settlement.

The history of the English Conquest is obscure. It occupied the 4th and 5th centuries (449-613) and ended with the invaders in firm possession of the whole Province with the exception of Cornwall, Wales and Cumberland where the remnant of the Roman-British population maintained independent kingdoms.

The English Conquest is important in that it destroyed the Roman civilisation in Britain, and established the English race and nation with its distinctive society, language, institutions and government. The early invaders were pagans greatly inferior to the Romans, but their conversion to Christianity (597-664) led steadily to a marked improvement in their civilisation. Owing to England's insular position, cultural progress during the period was mainly due to the Christian Church. Its efficient organisation ably assisted the civil governments, instituted maturer systems of law and justice, fostered both religious and secular learning, and greatly encouraged craftsmanship and the arts, especially literature and music. Proof of its success in aiding the material progress of the English is expressed in the work of a long line of eminent men of whom the most notable are Caedmon the poet who died in 680, Benedict Biscop the traveller, (638-690), Bede the teacher and historian (673-735), Alcuin the scholar (735-804), Wilfred, Archbishop of York (630-709), Alfred the Great (849-901), and Dunstan the churchman, scholar and statesman (960-988).

Social and cultural progress was retarded, though national unity was aided, by the stubborn struggle for supremacy waged between the Anglo-Saxon kingdoms during the period following settlement (613-829), and which resulted in the consolidation of the kingdoms of Northumbria, Mercia and Wessex. The end of the period was marked by the incursions of the pagan Danes or Vikings who overran the whole of England except Wessex which kingdom after a long struggle (797-900) maintained its independence under Alfred the Great, whose work made it possible for his successors, Edward, Athelstan and Edgar to subdue and anglicise the Danes, and to unite Wessex and the Danish kingdoms into the single kingdom of England (900-975).

The incapacity of Edgar's successors, Edward and Ethelred led to a renewal of the Danish invasions (979), the Danish Conquest of England under Sweyn (1002-13) and the establishment of a Danish dynasty with the accession of his son Canute as King of all England (1017-35), a period important in that it helped to unite the people under one head.

In 1042 the English dynasty was restored in the person of Edward the Confessor, but the active work of government was carried on by Godwin, Earl of Wessex, and his son Harold who, after becoming King in 1066, was in the same year defeated and killed at Hastings in battle against the invading Normans under William the Conqueror.

In Anglo-Saxon times, agriculture was the chief business of the people. Crops of wheat, oats and barley were grown and cattle, pigs and sheep were reared, not by individual enterprise, but under a characteristic system in which each village community was responsible for the due sequence of agricultural operations in fields not permanently enclosed. Manufactures were mainly confined to the homes of the people, the universal craftsmen being the spinner, weaver, shoemaker, carpenter and smith. Trade, in spite of the rough state of society, increased after settlement, and there was also an extensive commerce with Ireland, France, Germany and Scandinavia, the principal ports being London, Chester, Bristol and Dover.

Dwellings varied according to the rank and wealth of their builders. The poorer classes lived in mere wattled huts; lesser nobles or thanes had substantial timber-built straw-thatched homesteads, while more influential nobles inhabited long, low halls surrounded by a large courtyard. Dress was of coarse, gaily-coloured cloth, the chief garment being a short cloak beneath which was a woollen tunic extending from neck to knee and gathered at the waist by a belt. Shoes and strips of cloth cross-gartered protected the legs and feet and a thick woollen cap was usually worn out of doors. Both sexes were inordinately fond of ornament and jewellery, chiefly rings, clasps, bracelets and necklaces of amber, jet and the precious metals.

Early English Settlement. showing the
Hall of the Chief.

The Folk Moot or Tribal Assembly.

English Nobles.

English Thegn or Warrior.

English Peasants.

Bronze Pins.

Bronze Bucket.

Combat with lance and dagger.

Silver Bowl.

Silver mounted Drinking-horn.

Coin of Alfred the Great.

Bone Comb.

St. Augustine's Chair. Canterbury Cathedral.

St. Martin's Church, Canterbury. A Roman Church, restored by St. Augustine.

St. Augustine. The first Archbishop of Canterbury. 597-604

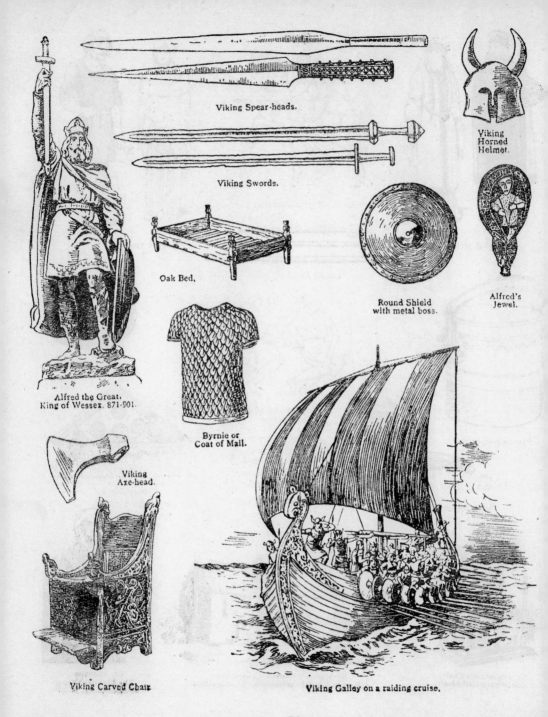

Viking Spear-heads.

Viking Swords.

Viking Horned Helmet.

Oak Bed.

Round Shield with metal boss.

Alfred's Jewel.

Alfred the Great, King of Wessex. 871-901.

Byrnie or Coat of Mail.

Viking Axe-head.

Viking Carved Chair.

Viking Galley on a raiding cruise.

14

Saxon Church, Bradford-on-Avon.
Built about A.D. 700.

Alfred makes peace with Guthrum, 878.

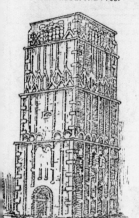

Saxon Tower.
Earl's Barton Church.
Northampton.

Saxon Font.

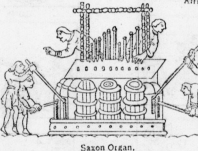

Saxon Organ.
Early 11th century.

St. Dunstan.
Statesman and
Primate. 960-988.

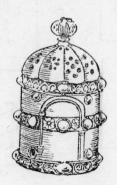

Saxon Lantern.

Viking Cross,
Oransay, Scotland.

JANUARY.   PLOUGHING.

FEBRUARY.   PRUNING TREES.

MARCH. BREAKING UP SOIL: DIGGING-SOWING-HARROWING

APRIL. FEASTING.

MAY. WATCHING SHEEP.

JUNE. CUTTING WOOD.

JULY. HAYMAKING.

AUGUST. HARVESTING.

SEPTEMBER. HUNTING-PASTURING SWINE.

OCTOBER   HAWKING.

NOVEMBER. GROUP ROUND A FIRE.

DECEMBER. THRESHING AND WINNOWING.

Country life as depicted in the Anglo-Saxon Calendar, 11th century.

4. MEDIAEVAL BRITAIN. 1066-1485.

The Norman Conquest (1066) was decisive; it inaugurated great and far-reaching changes in British history. The Normans were akin to the English, but they were more cultured and warlike and were gifted with greater capacities for organisation and government. They conserved all that was best in English institutions, related England with the continent, established a strong government under the Royal authority and thereby aided the foundation of a united nation. Owing to Britain's insularity the Normans gradually became one people with the English. The Norman kings relied mainly upon their English subjects; the speech of the people changed and was established as the English tongue, and distinctions between Normans and English at length disappeared.

The Norman or Early Mediaeval Period (1066-1154) is one of settlement after conquest. More advanced systems direct civil and religious government; social life is established on a feudal basis; trade and industry are intensified; finance, law and education are reformed, and the characteristic life of the English is regenerated by the influence of Norman ideas. The most notable development appears in architecture, the Norman genius being expressed in stone-built castles, abbeys and cathedrals, and in a style characterised chiefly by rude workmanship, massive walls and pillars and semi-circular arches. Fine existing examples are the White Tower of the Tower of London, the Keeps of Rochester, Norwich and Kenilworth Castles, the cathedrals of Durham and Norwich and the Abbeys of Tewkesbury and Furness.

The Angevin or Early Plantagenet Period (1154-1272) is important for the consolidation of the English nation, for the struggle for control between the civil and religious powers (Henry II. and Becket; John and Pope Innocent III.), and for that baronial struggle against the despotic pretensions of the Crown which apprenticed the nation in the arts of self-government. Henry II. reformed our political and judicial systems. Magna Carta (1215) established our national liberties. The work of Simon de Montfort (1208-65) founded our Imperial Parliament. Accordingly, the period produced a real English nation having its own institutions laws and language, strong enough to hold its place in the world and enterprising enough to grasp opportunities to expand.

The Later Plantagenet Period (1272-1485) is one of national expansion. Parliament was organised as a representative body with power to participate in government (1295). Edward I. effected the Conquest of Wales (1277-84) and attempted that of Scotland. In the Hundred Years' War, Edward III. (1327-77) and Henry V. (1413-22) sought to conquer France, their failure leading to the civil conflict of the Wars of the Roses (1455-85) which destroyed the power of the feudal nobles and established the despotic rule of the Tudors.

Socially, the Middle Ages saw the decay of Feudalism and the rise of the more law-abiding middle classes. Towns and cities grew in importance, industry was extended, trade and commerce were increased, and the law was strengthened into a Common Law enforced throughout the land. The loss of life in the French wars and the Black Death (1348) led to a social revolution which released many labourers from feudal services, converted large areas of corn land into enclosed pastures for sheep and greatly increased our commercial prosperity through the woollen industry. Also, the use of gunpowder revolutionised warfare and hastened the decay of feudalism. The religious teaching of John Wycliff (1320-84) and the Lollards was the prelude to the Reformation, while the poetry of Geoffrey Chaucer (1340-1400) and the introduction of the printing press by William Caxton (1476) prepared the way for the Revival of Learning and the new classical culture of the Renaissance.

By the fourteenth century towns also had grown rich through trade. Not only was wool shipped to Flanders and wine imported from Bordeaux, but fleets from Venice and Genoa brought luxuries from Egypt and Asia to the Cinque Ports and Southampton. Indeed, Englishmen were delighted with the rich eastern silks and velvets so bright and colourful, and with their light and gauzy linen and cotton cloths. In London the German merchants built wharves and warehouses, and the merchant-gild of Bristol owned fleets which traded even with Iceland. These were the merchant adventurers who owned their own ships and were jealous of any trade which went to the foreigner.

Within the town walls most houses were of wood, though a fine brick residence stood here and there, often ornamented with plaster decorations, glazed windows and red-tiled roof, while in the narrow, crooked streets of the poorer parts the cottages were merely hovels built of mud. Most houses were shops and factories as well as homes, with warehouse and workrooms on the ground floor and living and sleeping rooms above. On a bench in the porch goods made by the workmen were spread for passers-by to see and purchase, and over the front was hung a brightly painted sign. This golden arrow or blue boar's head represented the tradesman's name or craft, for though few could read, all could understand such signs and the most ignorant messenger could be trusted to find the Silver Axe in the Carpenters' Street, or the Three Lions by the East Gate, an inn whose jolly host was ready at any time to serve fish, fowl and meat to a multitude of travellers.

Norman Ship of Viking type with dragon prow and steerboard. (Bayeux Tapestry).

Anglo-Saxon warrior with typical round shield. Note his nasal-piece helmet and twice barbed spear.

Norman Knights storm and fire a city (Bayeux Tapestry). Note their body armour, nasal-piece helmets and kite-shaped shields.

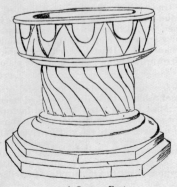

A 12th Century Font

An initial letter from an illuminated manuscript. Monks attained to rare skill. Designs were ornate and brightly coloured.

A Norman Warrior. Ringed-mail hauberk and nasal-piece helmet over mailed hood.

18

William the Conqueror,
1066-87. Founder of the
Norman Dynasty.

Seal of William I.

Doomsday Book.
Compiled 1086.

Norman
Swords.

Rochester Castle.
A typical Norman Keep.

The Keep, Norwich Castle.

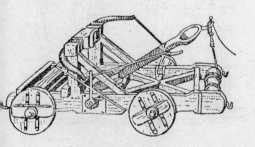

A Mangonel, a Norman siege engine.

A Battering Ram.

2164

A Norman noble wearing
tunic, over-tunic and
mantle.

Norman horsemen with lady riding pillion.

Villeins sowing and harrowing.

A Norman lady wearing
robe, mantle and head-veil.

Storing grain under the
direction of the bailiff.

Churning.

Women labourers in the field.

A Norman cruciform church with
characteristic semicircular arches.

A Norman Merchant-ship.

20

1. NORMAN CASTLE.

2. THE HALL.

3. THE BOWER.

Norman Bishop.

Norman Tower.
Tewkesbury Abbey.

St. Sepulchre's, Cambridge.
Built by Knights Templar.

Norman
Round
Tower.

Norman Staircase,
Canterbury Cathedral.

West Front, Tewkesbury Abbey.
Magnificent Norman Arch.

South Aisle, Ely Cathedral.

22

RICHARD I.

Richard I. 1189—1199. A prominent leader in the Third Crusade.

MURDER OF BECKET.

The murder of the Primate, Thomas Becket, in Canterbury Cathedral, 1170

KING JOHN

John. 1199—1216. His reign is important for the definition of our liberties in Magna Charta, 1215.

WHITEFRIAR (CARMELITE)

Carmelite or White Friar. The order was specially devoted to philanthropy.

SHIP OF TIME OF RICHARD I.

A 13th century Galley. Viking type with the addition of fore and stern castles.

A PREACHING FRIAR

A Dominican or Preaching Friar. The Order was specially devoted to combating heresy. Established in England in 1220.

A COUNTRY CART.

A Mediaeval Waggon. Used for the transport of household goods between manors.

Edward I., 1272—1307. Conquered Wales, 1277—83, and attempted the conquest of Scotland 1291—1307.

CONWAY CASTLE

Conway Castle. Built 1283 by Edward I. A castle of the stronghold type consisting of massive round towers connected by curtain walls.

QUARTER-STAFF

Quarter Staff. A popular mediaeval sport.

Robert Bruce. 1274—1329. Champion of Scotland against English aggression under Edwards I. and II

14th century armour. Brasses of Sir Ralph Bacon, 1320, and Sir John de Northwode, 1330.

24

13th century knights. Chain mail armour, the hauberk having a coif or hood under the close-fitting helmet. Features: long sleeves, mittens and leg-covering.

14th century knights. Mixed mail and plate armour with an emblazoned surcoat. Features: gauntlets, leg-pieces, camail and sugar-loaf helmets.

Interior architecture of a Norman Keep. Characteristics: rectangular structure, thick walls, narrow windows, defensive moat and gatehouse protected by portcullis and drawbridge.

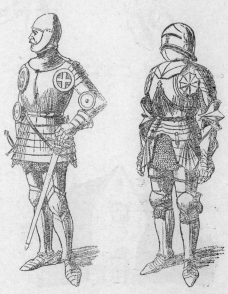

15th century knights. Complete plate armour, strong light and flexible.

ENGLISH ARCHER

An English Bowman.

John Wyclif, d. 1384. Leader of the Lollards and apostle of the English Reformation.

15th century armour. Perfectly fitting steel plates, light and flexible with graceful ridges and flutings to deflect weapon points.

14th century Ecclesiastical Architecture. Porch. St. Mary's Church, Beverley.

14th century Domestic Architecture. Old Houses at East Hendred, Berks.

Mailed Knights fighting in battle, 14th century. Note the two-edged broad-bladed sword with straight guard and blood channel.

14th century decorated capital. Conventional foliage design.

15th century Town House. Half-timber building with narrow front, carved beams and overhanging super-structure.

The Coronation chair made by order of Edward I. It contains the "Stone of Destiny" carried by Edward from Scone, Scotland in 1296.

Man at Arms. Type of light-armed, mobile troops forming the main body of infantry.

Costume in the 14th and 15th centuries. Materials rich. Styles full, florid and extravagant with profuse ornament.

A 15th century Miracle Play, the scenes in which were based upon the Miracles of Christ and the Saints.

Behind the Scene at a Mediaeval Miracle Play.

28

St. Joan of Arc, 1412—1431, the Saviour of France. Her relief of Orleans, 1429, foredoomed the English power in France.

An assault on the City walls by means of a siege tower.

A 14th century Bombard or Cannon.

A 15th century Cannon.

CAXTON'S PRINTING PRESS.

A moveable shed used in undermining a wall.

The first Printers. The Printing Press was first introduced into England in 1476 by William Caxton, 1422—1491.

5. TUDOR BRITAIN. 1485-1603.

In English history the year 1485 distinguishes the Modern Age from the Mediaeval ; the accession of Henry VII. coincides with Movements evolving a new civilisation.   Political, religious and social changes were imminent.   Foreign invasion and internal disruption from political anarchy and social unrest were potential dangers.   To guard against them the nation entrusted the Tudors with absolute authority.

Henry VII. (1485-1509) restored order after the Wars of the Roses, established the Rule of Law, repressed the feudal nobility, conserved the national finances and encouraged exploration and commerce.   He appreciated the changes due to the Renaissance which forced England to take an active part in European politics, and also the maritime discoveries of Bartholomew Diaz, Vasco da Gama, and Christopher Columbus, which stimulated commerce, increased national wealth and led European states to found Colonial Empires.

Henry VIII. (1509-47) was an enlightened statesman, despotic yet popular because his interests as a rule coincided with the nation's.   With the aid of Thomas Wolsey he raised England to a position of first importance by his ability in maintaining the balance of power in Europe and his recognition of the importance of sea power which led him to establish a powerful navy.   In 1529 political considerations arising from his divorce from Catherine of Aragon had momentous consequences.   Henry opposed the Papacy, made England independent of Rome, and took steps to found a national Church co-extensive with the State. In the Reformation Parliament (1529-36) he achieved drastic reforms including the acknowledgment of his spiritual supremacy, the abolition of payments and appeals to Rome and the destruction of the old system of monasticism.   Though Henry's policy was anti-papal his doctrines were anti-protestant, therefore he persecuted extremists of both persuasions.

Edward VI. (1547-53) was a young and weak King whose government was controlled by the protectorships of the Earls of Somerset (1547-49) and Northumberland (1549-53).   The work of Somerset is marked by his efforts to establish a more humane government, his support of Protestantism and the introduction of the Prayer Book (1549).   That of Northumberland was concerned mainly with the propagation of a more violent Protestantism and the unprincipled intrigues designed to secure the succession of the throne to Lady Jane Grey.

Mary (1553-58), who thwarted the schemes of Northumberland, reversed the policy of her predecessors. She restored the papal supremacy, and sacrificed England's political independence to Philip II. of Spain who by his marriage to Mary hoped to crush the Reformation.   Owing to her policy she was embroiled in revolts which led to the execution of Lady Jane Grey, in an outbreak of war with France resulting in the loss of Calais (1558), and in a vicious persecution of Protestants which made her rule infamous.

Elizabeth (1558-1603) was the greatest of the Tudors.   The success of her policy made England an independent insular State and established the Anglican Church as a National Church.   The Church of England was established by the Act of Supremacy and the Act of Uniformity (1559).   The Prayer Book of Edward VI. was restored (1559) and the Thirty-nine articles were authorised (1563).   Foreign policy was directed against the menaces of Scotland, France and Spain.   To counter their attacks Elizabeth supported the Protestant cause in Scotland and Flanders and encouraged the piratical attacks of adventurous seamen like Hawkins and Drake who sapped the strength of the Spanish Colonial Empire and ended the fear of invasion by their defeat of the Armada (1588).

Elizabeth's Age is also notable for the increased national prosperity.   Charters were granted to trading companies, e.g. the Muscovy, Levant and East India Companies.   Colonisation was attempted by settlements in Ireland and by the efforts of Sir Humphrey Gilbert and Sir Walter Raleigh to colonise Newfoundland and Virginia.   Trade and industry were assisted by monopolies intended to help new industries, by the protection afforded to refugee Protestant artisans from France and Flanders, and by the Statute of Apprentices (1563) which tried to regulate labour and wages.   In addition, the Poor Law (1601) was a notable attempt to minimise vagrancy.

The splendour of the Elizabethan Age is reflected in the advance in Literature and Learning.   Many Universities and Grammar Schools were founded.   The new Renaissance Style in Architecture was introduced.   Poetry and the Drama attained to inspiration, notably in the works of William Shakespeare (1564-1616), Edmund Spenser (1552-99), and Ben Jonson (1573- 1637).

Henry VII., 1485—1509. Founder of the Tudor dynasty and despotism.

The Chapel, Haddon Hall, Derbyshire. Timbered ceiling and Tudor or "Perpendicular" window.

A Tudor Schoolroom. The Renaissance gave a great impetus to classical learning.

Tudor Armour. Impractical in warfare; used only in jousts. Massive with chiselled, embossed and damascened surfaces richly engraved and gilt.

Anne Boleyn's Watch. A fine example of Tudor skill in constructive and decorative craftsmanship.

A Tudor Printing Press. Publications were chiefly translations of Greek and Latin Books.

Ferdinand Magellan's ship, "Victoria" The first to voyage round the world. 1519—22.

Tudor wood-carving, an art which attained its height under Elizabeth.

The "Great Harry," the most powerful Tudor battleship.
Built by Henry VIII., 1515.

Henry VIII., 1509-47.
Enlightened, accomplished and popular.
Notable for his despotic rule and his
advanced foreign and religious policies.

Sir Thomas More, 1478-1535.
Philosopher, Statesman
and Reformer.

Catherine of Aragon,
Queen of Henry VIII.

Hampton Court Palace erected by Cardinal Wolsey

Thomas Wolsey, 1475-1530.

Jousting, a favourite exercise of Tudor gentlemen.

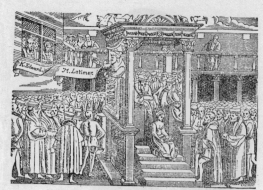

Bishop Latimer preaching before Edward VI.

A Palace of Francis I. A notable example of the Renaissance Architecture introduced into England under the Tudors.

Official under Henry VII. Revival of Simplicity and utility in dress.

A Tudor Bedroom with massive four-post bed and richly carved furniture.

Lady Jane Grey's cell in the Tower of London.

Edward VI, 1547-53.

Queen Mary, 1553-58.

A Shilling of Edward VI.

A Penny of Edward VI.

The Martyrs' Memorial, Oxford.
Erected to commemorate the martyrdom
of Bishops Ridley and Latimer, 1555, and
Archbishop Cranmer, 1556.

Tudor Dress.

Thomas Cranmer, 1489-1556.
Archbishop of Canterbury, 1533.

Early Tudor Musketeer and Pikeman.

A Spanish Galleon.

The Earl of Essex, 1567-1601. Favourite of Elizabeth.

Sir Francis Drake, 1540-96.

A Street Watchman.

Queen Elizabeth, 1558-1608.

A London Water-Carrier.

The Birthplace of William Shakespeare, Stratford-on-Avon. A typical Tudor cottage still well preserved.

An Elizabethan Manor House.

Mary Stuart, 1542-87.
Queen of Scots, 1542-67.

The Birthplace of John Knox at Gifford Gate, Haddington.

John Knox, 1513-72.

Mary, Queen of Scots enters Holyrood on her arrival from France in 1561.

Loch Leven Castle

Holyrood Palace, founded by David I. in 1128

Smithfield. The place of martyrdom of the London
Protestants condemned under Mary, 1555.

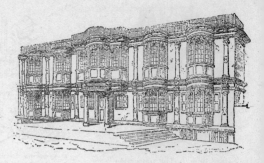

The Old Palace, Greenwich, a favourite residence
of Queen Elizabeth.

Elizabeth's State Coach.

A Tudor Tankard.

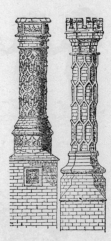

Tudor Decorated Chimneys.
Graceful and richly ornamented.

The Earl of Leicester, 1532
—88. General and Courtier.
under Elizabeth.

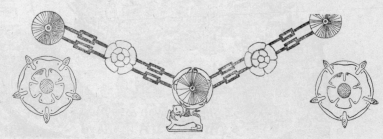

Ornament combining white and red roses symbolic of the Union of York and Lancaster.
Henry VII. married Elizabeth of York, 1486.

37

A Chained Bible. The translation of Miles Coverdale was the first authorised by Henry VIII. for use in parish churches, 1539.

A Weaving Loom. Weaving was the staple English industry from the 13th century.

Costume of a noble under Edward VI. Features: full hose, puffed Sleeves and flat cap.

Mummers, or entertainers at Old English country revels

Henry VIII. embarks at Dover for the field of the Cloth of Gold, 1520. Note the types of warships and defences.

The "Ark Royal," a warship in Elizabeth's navy.

Thomas Cromwell, 1485—1540. The "Hammer of the Monks," who carried out the Dissolution of the Monasteries, 1535—40.

Tudor vagrants. Unemployment was a grave social problem. It was partly solved by the Elizabethan Poor Law, 1601.

Tudor Heavy Artillery. "A Piece of Cannon," 1590.

Sir Walter Raleigh, 1552—1616. Statesman, Courtier and Navigator.

The Old Globe Theatre in Southwark, Notable for the original production of Shakespeare's Plays.

Hugh Latimer. 1485—1555. Protestant Reformer and Martyr, Bishop of Worcester.

Westminster Hall, founded by William II.
The scene of important State Trials.

Queen Elizabeth makes a State Progress through London.
Note the dress of the period.

The fight with the Armada, 1588. The Spanish fleet was destroyed by storm after
its repulse by the navy under Admirals Lord Howard and Sir Francis Drake.

Elizabethan dress. Rich material;
extravagant but picturesque in
style.

6. STUART BRITAIN. 1603-1714.

Outstanding features of the 17th century are the struggle for civil and religious liberty waged between the King and Parliament, and the foundation of the British Empire by colonisation in North America. The Stuarts threatened national liberty by asserting the " Divine Right of Kings," a doctrine purporting to make the sovereign independent of Parliament and superior to the law. In 1604 Parliament asserted its right to share the responsibilities of government. In 1621 it revived Impeachment in vindication of its right to control the King's ministers. In 1642 it declared war in its determination to establish itself as the governing body in the state. In effect neither was wholly successful. Parliamentary absolutism did not replace Royal absolutism. The execution of Charles I. (1649) forced the Crown to govern through responsible ministers ; and though the Revolution of 1688 made Parliament a permanent part of the machinery of government, it did not assume the work of government.

James I. was the first ruler of both England and Scotland. He had exaggerated ideas respecting the royal prerogative ; his civil government was arbitrary and he did not understand the value of popular support. His foreign policy was impolitic ; his attitude towards the religious controversy was disastrous. As he failed to conciliate public opinion his reign proved the prelude to the revolution against his son, Charles I.

Charles I. (1625-49) was also obsessed with ideas of absolutism and therefore resisted all attempts of the Commons to participate in government. The Commons determined to maintain a parliamentary constitution but Charles ruled as a despot, his civil and religious policies respectively being directed by Thomas Wentworth, Earl of Strafford and William Laud, Archbishop of Canterbury. In lieu of Acts of Parliament proclamations were issued, the judges were in a state of subservience, and the privileged courts of Star Chamber and High Commission maintained a reign of terror. In 1640 a financial crisis due to the failure of his Scottish Wars forced Charles to summon Parliament whereupon the struggle between them was renewed with increasing bitterness until the outbreak of the Civil War (1642-49) waged to decide who should rule, King or Parliament. The military success of Parliament and the execution of Charles I. (1649) concentrated power in the hands of Oliver Cromwell. His aim was to establish a form of government in which the nation would be ruled by its elected representatives. In form his government was a republic ; in fact it was a military despotism.

Charles II. (1660-85) was clever, but selfish and extravagant. His reign is important for the progress made in parliamentary government, as Parliament gained control over the King's ministers and the national finances, and increased its influence by its formation into two parties, theWhigs in opposition to the powers of the Crown, and the Tories who wished to maintain them. Also of importance were the growth of our colonial Empire in America, the maritime supremacy achieved by a successful war against the Dutch (1665), the Great Plague which ravaged London (1665) and the disastrous Fire which succeeded it (1666).

James II. (1685-88) aimed to be despotic and to restore England to Roman Catholicism. His pretensions led to a rebellion in favour of the Duke of Monmouth which was brutally suppressed, and to the " Glorious Revolution," (1688) which led to the flight of James II. to France and to the election to his throne of his daughter Mary and her husband, William of Orange. The Revolution was a national rising against Stuart absolutism. It maintained the Supremacy of the Law and founded our modern form of Parliamentary government by making possible ministerial and cabinet government.

Under William III. (1689-1702) rebellions in favour of the restoration of James II. were suppressed in Ireland and Scotland. In addition, England progressed as a maritime and commercial nation. Our colonies in North America were strengthened, commerce with India increased, and voyages of discovery began to open up the Pacific Ocean and the Continent of Australia.

Anne (1702-14) was a daughter of James II. Her reign is notable for the war waged in the Netherlands against France, and which resulted in the capture of Gibraltar (1704) and the victories of the Duke of Marlborough at Blenheim (1704), Ramillies (1706), Oudenarde (1708) and Malplaquet (1709). It was ended by the Treaty of Utrecht (1713) which established the supremacy of Britain in North America and formed the prelude to the 18th century struggle waged between France and Britain in America and India for colonial and commercial greatness. Even more notable was the political Union between England and Scotland achieved by the Act of Union (1707). By this Act the United Kingdom of Great Britain was established under a single government, Scotland being represented in Parliament by forty-five Members in the Commons and sixteen Peers in the Lords.

James VI. of Scotland and I. of England,
1603-25. Founder of the Stuart Dynasty.

The Gunpowder Plot Conspirators who attempted to blow up the
Houses of Parliament, 1605.

The Pilgrim Fathers land in Cape Cod Bay, Massachusetts,
1620, and found the New England Colonies in North America.

The "Mayflower" in which the Pilgrim Fathers
voyaged to America, 1620.

The House of the Gunpowder Plot Conspirators
at Lambeth

A 17th century country waggon.

Charles I. 1625-49, whose absolutism caused the Civil War, 1642, and his execution at Whitehall, 1649.

The Banqueting Hall, Whitehall, designed by Inigo Jones.

William Laud, 1573-1645. Primate, 1633. Executed for his support of Charles I., 1645.

A Puritan, characterised by extreme sobriety in habits and dress.

A Charles I. Shilling.

A Cavalier in armour.

John Hampden. 1594-1643. Notable for his refusal to pay Ship Money, 1638.

King Charles's Tower, Chester, from which Charles I. watched the Battle of Rowton Heath, 1645

Thomas Wentworth, Earl or Strafford, 1593-1641. Executed for supporting the absolutism of Charles I

Oliver Cromwell, 1599—1658. Lord Protector of the Commonwealth, 1653—58.

John Pym, 1584-1643. Parliamentary Leader against the pretensions of Charles I.

The Defence of Lathom House by the Countess of Derby against the forces of the Parliament, 1644.

The St. Lawrence Gate, Drogheda. The city garrison was massacred after capitulation to Cromwell, 1649.

Admiral Blake. 1597-1657 Notable for his victories against the Dutch, 1652-54.

An Ironside, or soldier of the disciplined troop raised by Oliver Cromwell, 1643.

A pikeman, the type of soldier forming the main body of infantry 1642-49.

Carisbrooke Castle, Isle of Wight, where Charles I, was imprisoned, 1647.

Samuel Pepys, 1633-1703.
A notable diarist.

The "Royal Charles," a warship
of the type used against the Dutch.

The Earl of Clarendon, 1609-1674.
Notable for the Clarendon Code,
enactments against Nonconformity.

Charles II., 1660-85. His reign
was notable for Colonial expansion
and the progress of Parliament.

A London Street in the time
of the Great Plague, 1665.

Charles II. received by General
Monk on his landing at Dover, 1660.

Old St. Paul's, London. Built during the 13th and
14th centuries and destroyed by the Fire, 1666.

Sir Christopher Wren, 1632-1723. The
famous architect who designed St. Paul's
Cathedral, London.

45

James II., 1685-88, whose despotism
precipitated the
"Glorious Revolution," 1688.

The Traitors Gate, Tower of London.

Halberds. or Pikes.

Horse Armour used under
the Stuarts.

A Stuart Musketeer. The musket
was cumbersome, unreliable and
of little practical service.

A Royalist or Cavalier whose dress
expresses extreme luxury.

The escape of the Duke of Monmouth from Sedgemoor, 1685.

William III., 1689-1702. Appointed King by Act of Parliament upon the deposition of James II.

Chelsea Hospital. Founded by Charles II. for invalid soldiers. Architect, Sir Christopher Wren.

Blenheim Palace. The National Gift to the Duke of Marlborough, rewarding his successes in the War of the Spanish Succession, 1702-1713. Architect, Sir Christopher Wren.

Queen Anne, 1702-1714. Daughter of James II. and last Stuart sovereign.

London Watchmen. Their chief duty was to guard against fire.

Interior of the Swan Theatre, London, in the late 17th century.

47

The Mace of the House of Commons. A new Head and Base were made in 1660.

A Dragoon or Mounted Infantryman, trained and armed to fight either on horseback or on foot, 1642-49.

Front of a 17th Century London House.

The Title-piece of a Commonwealth Newspaper. It reported Parliamentary enactments and proceedings.

A 17th Century Coach.

Helmets used during the Civil War, 1642-49.

The "Half Moon," in which Henry Hudson discovered and explored the Hudson River, 1609.

48

A London Trained Band Soldier.
1642-49.

A 17th Century Country Woman.

Inigo Jones, 1573-1651. Foremost
Architect under the Early Stuarts.

ANOLDO CAR REGIS
1633   9
IF STONES COVLD SPEAKE
THEN LONDONS PRAYSE
SVOVLD SOVNDE WHO
BVILT THIS CHVRCH AND
CITTIE FROM THE GROVNDE
VAUGHAN AED

Tablet in Londonderry Cathedral
commemorating the founding of
the city, 1633.

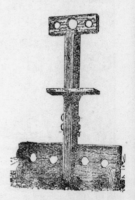

The Stocks and Pillory. A severe
mode of punishment in that prison-
ers were open to public ill-treatment.

Lady of the time of James I.
Full skirts, high-crowned hat,
linen ruffles, lace embroidery.

Monument commemor-
ating the Battle of the
Boyne, 1690.

A Hackney Coachman.

Monument commemorating
the Siege of Londonderry
1689.

49

THE HOVSE OF LORDS

THE HOVSE OF COMMONS

The Houses of Parliament as they assembled under Queen Anne, 1702-14

A gentleman of William III.'s reign. A compromise between Cavalier extravagance and Puritan simplicity.

A gentleman of Anne's reign. Note the development of the wig.

A 17th century Farm House.

a Taylor

A London Tailor

A 17th century Yeoman Farmer.

A 17th century Fire Engine

7. HANOVERIAN BRITAIN. 1714-1820.

The Hanoverian Dynasty was founded by George I., Elector of Hanover, whose right to the British throne was established by the Act of Succession, 1701. The important political events in this period were the ascendancy of the Whig Party under the leadership notably of Robert Walpole (1721-42) and William Pitt, Earl of Chatham (1756-61) ; the Scottish Rebellions in 1715 and 1745 to restore the Stuarts ; the struggle between Britain and France (1739-1815) in Europe, America and India for colonial and commercial supremacy, and the War of American Independence (1775-83) which revolutionised British colonial policy.

Manufactures rose slowly but steadily until the reign of George III. (1760) when a series of discoveries introduced the Industrial Revolution which increased production, stimulated the cotton trade and completely changed the social life of the nation. Notable inventions were James Hargreaves' Spinning Jenny (1770), Richard Arkwright's Water Frame (1771), Samuel Crompton's Spinning Mule (1779) and Edward Cartwright's Power Loom (1784) which enabled weaving operations to keep pace with those of spinning. Meanwhile James Watt improved the Steam Engine ; John Roebuck developed iron by the use of coal for smelting ; Josiah Wedgwood gave a new impetus to pottery manufacture, and in almost every trade it became possible to produce more and at a cheaper rate.

An Agrarian Revolution proceeded simultaneously with the Industrial Revolution. Improved methods and appliances and the needs of the increased industrial population concentrating in large towns revolutionised husbandry and augmented the food supply. Large farms replaced small holdings ; the capitalist farmer arose ; breeds of cattle and sheep were improved ; and a series of Enclosure Acts began in 1760 which made nearly all common lands proprietary. These conditions increased the prosperity of landowners, but they bore hardly on the bulk of the rural population who became labourers. In towns also, the factory system and the high prices, especially after the Revolutionary and Napoleonic Wars (1792-1815), so increased pauperism that in the early 19th century one seventh of the population was in receipt of poor-law relief.

The 18th century saw a mental as well as a material revolution. The old religious passions faded, and an " Age of Reason " arose in which religion was saved from decay mainly by the work of the Oxford Society or Methodists. Under the enthusiastic leadership of John Wesley (1703-91) the Methodists created a widespread religious revival and eventually became organised into a large and well-governed community, the Methodist Church. In addition, a striking feature of religious life was the Evangelical Movement which produced no new Church but influenced all existing ones. It led to a stronger sense of personal religion, zeal and philanthropy, and resulted in the foundation of missionary societies, the Bible Society, and Sunday schools. Leaders of the movement were William Cowper, the reformer of English Poetry, John Howard, the reformer of prison abuses, and William Wilberforce, eminent for his efforts to secure the abolition of slavery.

Early in the 18th century, Architecture greatly declined, though other Arts improved. A national English school of painting, foreshadowed by the genius of William Hogarth, was founded by Sir Joshua Reynolds (1732-92). Music received a new impetus from the direction of Frederick Handel, the great master of Oratorio, and the standard of Literature, both poetry and prose, steadily advanced, especially after the middle of the century.

Few schools existed in the eighteenth century. For the sons of the wealthy there were several famous public schools such as Eton, and those attached to cathedrals such as St. Paul's in London and St. Peter's in York. In some old towns there were also certain " Grammar Schools," founded in Tudor times, where hard-working boys spent very long hours learning Latin and Greek, in which process both bright and dull received innumerable whippings. Upon leaving these schools youths usually went to the University of Oxford or Cambridge where they never troubled to learn unless they were naturally studious. Since tutors rarely taught and professors gave few lectures, the undergraduates under their charge lived as they liked. Indoors they drank and gambled, and for outdoor recreation delighted in cock-fighting, duelling, boxing and driving " post " to London. Held in low esteem on this account, the universities were noted for rowdyism and political agitation rather than for learning. Towards the end of the century, however, they too awakened from " sleep," and instituted reforms which made them so famous for teaching and scholarship that they have ever since attracted students from all parts of the world.

George I. 1714-27. Founder of the Hanoverian Dynasty. Succeeded under the Act of Succession, 1701.

A typical country mansion in the 18th century.

The Duke of Cumberland. He defeated the Jacobites at Culloden, Scotland, 1746.

Leather Jacks and Candlesticks.

A Georgian Squire. Typical country landowner and magistrate.

Sailors arresting smugglers. Smuggling reached its height in the 18th century, gangs being lawless and defiant.

A Georgian "Dandy." Note the sword carried for defence.

James Edward Stuart, 1688-1766, the Old Pretender, son of James II, and leader of the Jacobites, 1715.

Dress of a Lady under Georges I. and II.

A London Merchant for whom the Hanoverian Succession opened a new era of prosperity.

Charles Edward Stuart, 1720-88, the Young Pretender, grandson of James II and leader of the Jacobites, 1745.

George II., 1727-60.

A Sedan Chair, the chief street conveyance in 17th and 18th centuries.

Admiral Vernon, 1684-1757. Captured Portobello in the war against Spain, 1739.

A Sepoy or British trained native soldier employed in British service in India.

A Naval Seaman, early 18th century. Most sailors were pressed into the Service.

A North American Indian. The tribes were vicious enemies of the early British settlers in New England.

A Foot Soldier. Dress and equipment, 1759. Note the variety of Weapons.

Sir Robert Walpole, 1676-1745. Statesman and Financier. Premier, 1721-42.

Joseph Dupleix, 1697-1763. French Governor in India and Chief opponent of Robert Clive.

William Pitt, Earl of Chatham. 1708-78. The "Great Commoner."

Lord Clive, 1725-74. Founder of the British Empire in India.

George III., 1760-1820. His reign is notable for the wars against France, the Agrarian and Industrial Revolutions and the loss of the American Colonies.

Children working in a coal mine. The exploitation of child labour was the worst feature of 18th century industrial development.

The first Spinning Machine. The spinning jenny invented by James Hargreaves, 1764.

Lexington, the first battle in the war of American Independence. 1775.

Samuel Johnson, 1709-84. Scholar lexicographer and author. He compiled the first English Dictionary.

Country Gentleman in George III.'s reign.

The Death of Captain Cook upon landing in the Sandwich Islands, 1779.

Ploughing. Improved implements developed rapidly in the 18th century.

Warren Hastings, 1732-1818. A notable administrator and first Governor-General of India, 1774-85.

George Frederick Handel, 1685-1759. Foremost musician and composer renowned as the "Master of Oratorio."

Arthur Young, 1741-1820. He advocated the reform of Agriculture by Enclosures and by improved methods in cultivation.

Captain James Cook, 1728-79. Famous for his exploration of the coasts of New Zealand and Australia.

Richard Arkwright, 1732-92. The first to apply water power to the driving of spinning machinery.

The Steam Pumping Engine, invented by Thomas Newcommen 1705. Its inefficiency suggested the improvements of James Watt.

James Brindley, 1716-72. The first great canal engineer. Constructor of the Bridgewater Canal, 1761.

James Wolfe, 1727-59. Founder of the British Empire in Canada.

The Spinning Mule invented by Samuel Crompton, 1779. An improved power machine which increased enormously the production of thread.

James Watt, 1736-1819 inventor of the first effective steam engine, 1769.

A Lady in the reign of George III.

A typical 18th century town house

A Highlander, typical of those enlisted by William Pitt to found the famous Highland Regiments.

William Pitt the Younger, 1759-1806. Statesman and Orator. Premier, 1783-1801, 1804-06.

Death of Nelson at the Battle of Trafalgar, 1805.

The Duke of Wellington, 1769-1852. General and Statesman. Famous for his Peninsular War campaigns, 1808-14, and his victory at Waterloo, 1815.

Lord Nelson, 1758-1805. Admiral, notable for his victories at the Nile, 1798 ; Copenhagen, 1801 and Trafalgar, 1805.

H.M.S. Victory, Lord Nelson's Flag Ship at Trafalgar. A Typical "Wooden Wall" of Old England.

Napoleon Bonaparte. 1769-1821. General and first Emperor of the French. His ambitions proved a menace to British security, 1793-1815.

Foot Soldier in dress and equipment of the period 1806-15.

A Dandy at the end of George III.'s reign.

Infantryman, period of the Peninsular War, 1808-14.

A "peeler," or member of the Metropolitan Police Force founded by Sir Robert Peel, 1829.

A Farmer, 1780-1815, the most prosperous years for agriculture.

8. MODERN BRITAIN.

The Modern Period comprising the 19th and 20th centuries is politically important for the triumph of Democratic Government, in which government is controlled by the representatives of the whole people, not merely of one class, and for the adoption of national principles in legislation.

In 1832 the Reform Act improved representation in the Commons by a distribution of seats, and extended the franchise to tenant and householding classes as well as to landowners. Later Reform Acts, notably in 1867 and 1884, further extended the franchise until in 1928 the Representation of the People Act entitled all adult citizens of both sexes to vote in Parliamentary and Local Government elections. In addition, Parliament has assumed responsibility for the welfare and protection of all classes in society, a condition emphasised by the supervision of Local Authorities by Government Departments, and by such Social Legislation as the Factory, Education, Insurance, Housing Acts, etc.

An important development in the period is the expansion of the British Empire throughout the world. This has led to an advanced world civilisation, an ample source of supply of food and raw materials, an outlet for surplus population and an increase in national enterprise and wealth. Colonial expansion also confirmed the future development of Britain as an industrial rather than agricultural nation, and by the grant of responsible government to the colonies, created the British Commonwealth of Nations.

Striking features of the period are the progress in exploration and discovery, the improvements in the means of transport and communication, the elaboration of machinery, and the increase in scientific knowledge all of which have extended the material prosperity of the nation. The application of modern scientific and philosophic thought has increased working-class comfort, wealth and longevity, engendered political changes by educating the democracy, improved the standard of living of all classes, revolutionised the conditions of labour and wages and reorganised society.

The 20th century opened a new era. The state has become omni-competent in that it controls or influences nearly all the activities of citizens. In politics, the principles of Nationality and Political Freedom have triumphed as may be seen in the grant of responsible government to British Colonies, in the acknowledgment, by Home Rule, of an Irish Nation, and the adoption, since 1918, of Constitutional Government in all European states. In addition, Internationalism has become a feature of the Age. Both Capital and Labour have international interests, and national activities, such as those of the Post Office, have international applications. Also, the trend in education through the medium of the universities, and the trend in politics, by the establishment of the League of Nations and the holding of Congresses and Conferences is to promote international co-operation rather than to maintain a national isolation.

Inventions, discoveries and reforms naturally led to startling changes in English social life during the nineteenth century. To-day, with few exceptions, all classes are wealthier, healthier and happier than a hundred years ago, while the working man particularly is better housed, fed and clothed, better educated and skilled, better fitted to master his work and to enjoy his recreation and more ambitious for himself and his children.

It is impossible to describe the numberless changes that have transformed our lives and habits within the last century. Gas was first used in London in 1812, but electric light is now replacing it. In 1829 the first railway was opened, but petrol has now made the highroads busier transport arteries than are the railroads, and airways services are steadily increasing in utility and importance.

For fifty years inventors have amazed us by their skill : small things as well as great have added to our comfort. Our great-grandfathers had no matches ; they lighted their fires and candles from tinder, flint and steel. Farmers had neither self-binders nor motor ploughs and business men had neither typewriters nor telephones. Mothers had no labour-saving sewing machines and electric cookers : fathers had no motor cars and no wireless, and children had no good schools, no free libraries and no public parks. Then the poor were poor indeed since workmen dwelt in hovels, and women and children suffered in mines and toiled long hours in unhealthy factories. Food was costly, work was slavery and wages were a mere pittance.

George IV., 1820-30. His reign inaugurated an era of political and social reform.

The Stage Coach, the principal vehicle of travel before the advent of the railway.

William IV., 1830-37. His reign is notable for the reform of the House of Commons, 1832.

Arctic Expedition, 1829, under Sir John Ross who planted the British Flag on the North Magnetic Pole.

Prosperous middle class merchant or industrialist, period of William IV.

A Dame School in the early 19th century.

Country Squire or landowner, period of George IV

George Canning, 1770-1827. Statesman and founder of the "New Toryism" favouring social reforms.

Sir John Moore, 1761-1809. Commander in the Peninsular War, and famous for his successful Retreat to Corunna 1809

Edmund Burke, 1729-97. Statesman, Orator and Author. Notable for his attitude towards the French Revolution.

John Wesley, 1703-91. Religious Reformer and founder of the Methodist Church.

Queen Victoria, 1837-1901, whose reign is notable for the growth of democratic government.

British Warships bombarding Mombasa, an East African centre of the Slave Trade.

Lady in the dress of the early Victorian Period, 1840.

The murder of Bishop James Hannington, 1885, by natives of Uganda.

Lady, 1860, wearing the crinoline, a skirt supported by a series of hoops.

Sir Rowland Hill, 1795-1879. Notable for his introduction in 1840 of Penny Postage.

Sir Robert Peel. 1788-1850. Premier, 1834-35, 1841-46. Notable for his Repeal of the Corn Laws, 1846.

Richard Cobden, 1804-65. Statesman and Economist. Famous for his advocacy of Free Trade

Lord Shaftesbury, 1801-85. Statesman and Social Reformer whose efforts led to the First Factory Act, 1833

George Stephenson, 1781-1848. The first famous **Locomotive** and **Railway** **Engineer**.

An early Railway Train. The first Railways constructed in England were the Stockton and Darlington Railway, 1825, and the Liverpool and Manchester Railway, 1830.

The "Great Eastern," a pioneer iron steamship built for the Atlantic Service. Being underpowered she proved a failure and subsequently became a cable laying ship.

William Wilberforce, 1759-1833. Reformer and Philanthropist, notable for his efforts to abolish slavery.

Charles Dickens, 1812-70. **Famous** Novelist, whose writings depict the social life of his time.

The "Comet," built in 1812 by Henry Bell, the first passenger steamer to run on the Clyde.

William Makepeace **Thackeray**, 1811-63. Famous Novelist.

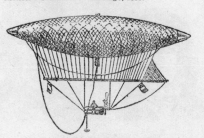

Rickett's Steam Road-Carriage, 1860.

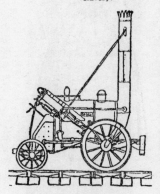

The "Rocket," designed by George Stephenson, 1829.

Charles Darwin, 1309-82. **Naturalist** and propounder of the Theory of Evolution.

Henri Giffard's steam-driven Airship, constructed in 1851.

Michael Faraday, 1791-1867. Chemist and Physicist. Famous for his electrical research.

Sir James Outram, 1803-63. General in India, who succeeded in relieving Lucknow 1857.

David Livingstone, 1813-77, exploring in the heart of Africa

Infantryman, period of the Crimean War. 1854-56

A Montgolfier Hot Air Balloon, 1783, a pioneer of aerial flight.

Charles Sturt, d. 1869 exploring the River Murray, Australia.

Florence Nightingale, 1820-1910. Notable for her self-sacrificing care of the wounded in the Crimea.

Field-Marshal Lord Roberts, 1832-1914. Commander in the Afghan War, 1878-80, and the Boer War, 1899-1902.

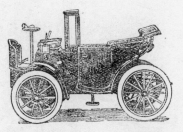

An early Motor Car. The first internal combustion engine was designed in 1885 by Gottlieb Daimler, a German inventor.

An early Hand-Pump Fire Engine.

William Ewart Gladstone, 1809-1898. Statesman. The "Grand Old Man" of British Politics

Cantilever Bridge spanning the River St. Lawrence at Quebec
A modern engineering triumph. Opened 1917.

Lord Beaconsfield, 1804-81. Statesman and Author Premier 1868, 1874-80.

A Maori, or native of New Zealand.

Cecil Rhodes, 1853-1902. Administrator and Empire Builder in South Africa. Pioneer in the development of Rhodesia.

General Charles Gordon, 1833-85. Killed at Khartum, while engaged in suppressing the Arab slave trade.

Kaffirs, or Native Negroes of South Africa.

The Government Buildings at Delhi, the political capital of India.

British Soldiers fighting against the Zulus at Rorke's Drift, 1879.

The Zulu advance at Kambula Hill, 1879.

62

Edward VII., 1901-10. He established the Entente between England and France, 1904.

The first Biplane. In this machine Wilbur and Orville Wright in 1903, first accomplished a sustained flight.

George V., b. 1865. Succeeded 1910. Notable for the democratic spirit which has characterised his rule.

Admiral Lord Jellicoe, b. 1859. In command of the British High Seas Fleet. 1914-18.

H.M.S. Lion. Typical Modern Battle Cruiser. Flagship of Admiral Beatty, Battle of Jutland, 1916.

A Modern Soldier in fighting kit

Admiral Lord Beatty, b. 1871. Notable for his successes at Heligoland Bight, Dogger Bank and Jutland, 1916.

Lord Oxford and Asquith 1852-1928. Premier, 1908-1916.

Camouflage. During the Great War, ships were strangely painted in order to break the sharp outlines which made them easy victims for submarines.

Field Marshal Earl Kitchener, 1850-1916. Notable for his successful organisation during the Great War.

The Supermarine-Napier "S.5." first Schneider Cup Race Winner. Average speed for 217 miles course was 281 miles per hour.

Field Marshal Lord Ypres, 1852-1925. In command of the British Armies in France. 1914-15.

A Modern Siege Howitzer used for the long range bombardment of fortified positions.

A Tank, a British War Weapon first used in 1915.

The late Sir Henry Segrave's "Sunbeam," the first car to attain a speed of more than 200 miles per hour

The Cenotaph at Whitehall. London

A Modern British Submarine.

A.S.